On a Beam of Light

chronicle books·san francisco

A Story of Albert Einstein by Jennifer Berne   pictures by Vladimir Radunsky

Over 100 years ago, as the stars swirled in the sky, as the Earth circled the sun, as the March winds blew through a little town by a river, a baby boy was born. His parents named him Albert.

Albert turned one year old. And didn't say a word.

Albert turned two. And didn't say a word.

Albert turned three. And hardly said a word at all.

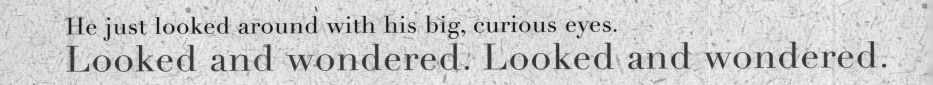

He just looked around with his big, curious eyes.
Looked and wondered. Looked and wondered.

His parents worried. Little Albert was so different; was there something wrong? But he was their baby, so they loved him . . . no matter what.

One day, when Albert was sick in bed, his father brought him
a compass—a small round case with a magnetic needle inside.
No matter which way Albert turned the compass, the needle always
pointed north, as if held by an invisible hand. Albert was so amazed
his body trembled.
Suddenly he knew there were mysteries in the world—hidden and silent, unknown and unseen.
He wanted, more than anything, to understand those mysteries.

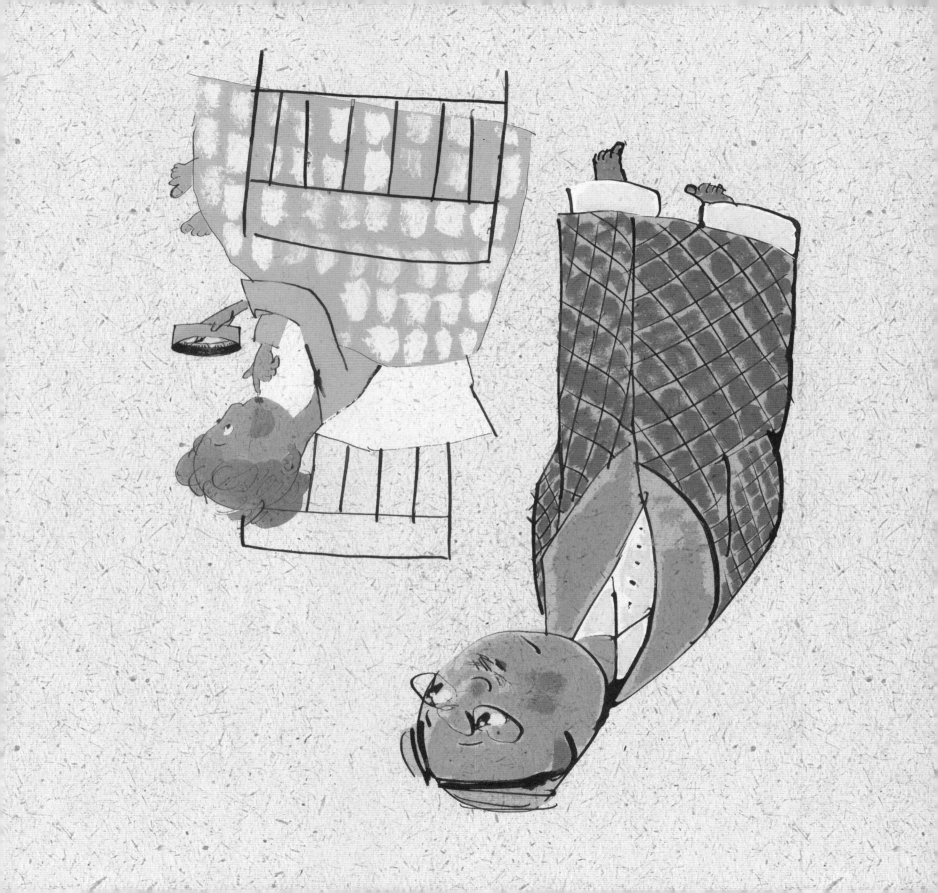

Albert started asking questions. Questions at home. Questions at school. So many questions that some of his teachers told him he was a disruption to his class. They said he would never amount to anything unless he learned to behave like all the other students.

But Albert didn't want to be like the other students.

He wanted to discover the hidden mysteries in the world.

One day, as Albert was zipping through the countryside on his bicycle, he looked up at the beams of sunlight speeding from the sun to the Earth. He wondered, what would it be like to ride one of those beams? And in his mind, right then and there, Albert was no longer on his bicycle, no longer on the country road . . . he was racing through space on a beam of light. It was the biggest, most exciting thought Albert had ever had. And it filled his mind with questions.

Albert began to read and study.

He read about light and sound. About heat and magnetism. And about gravity, the invisible force that pulls us down toward our planet, and keeps the moon from floating away into outer space.

MAGNETISM
GRAVITY
LIGHT
SOUND

And he read about numbers. Albert loved numbers.
They were like a secret language for figuring things out. But all that
reading still didn't answer all of Albert's questions. So he kept on
reading. Wondering. And learning.

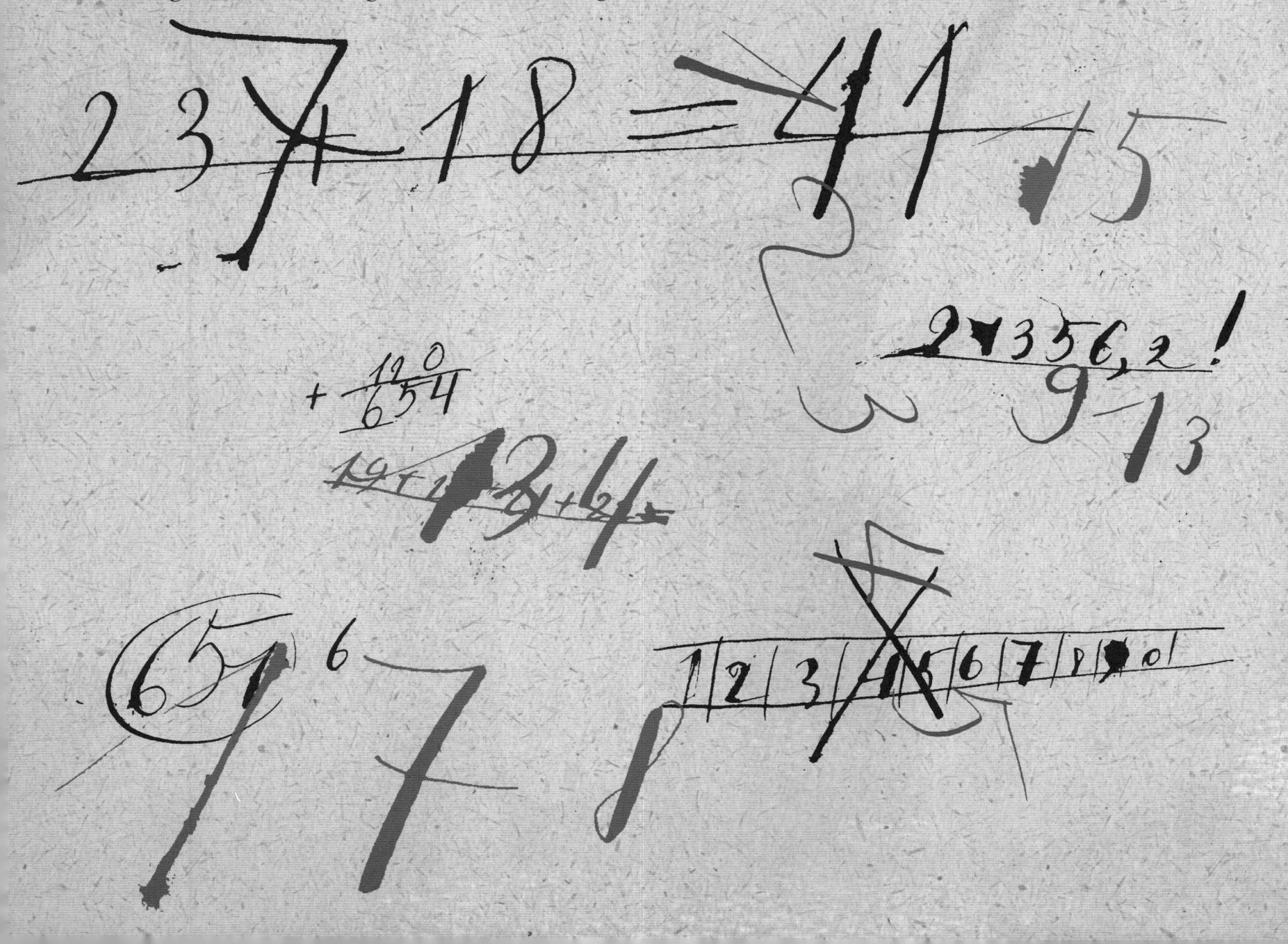

When Albert graduated from college, he wanted to teach the subjects
he loved—all the things he had read about all those years.
But Albert couldn't find a job as a teacher.
So he got another job.

A simple, quiet job in a government office. An office where he worked with other people's ideas and inventions. He did his work very well and very quickly . . . so quickly that he had lots of extra time to think and wonder.

GOVERNMENT OFFICE

Albert watched a lump of sugar dissolve and disappear into his hot tea.
How could this happen?

He watched the smoke from his pipe swirl and disappear into the air.
How could one thing disappear into another?

Then he began to figure it out. He thought about the idea that everything is made out of teeny, tiny, moving bits of stuff—far too tiny to see—little bits called "atoms." Some people didn't believe that atoms existed, but Albert's figuring helped prove that **everything in the world is made of atoms . . .** even sugar and tea, even smoke and air. Even Albert and you.

Even this Book is mAde of Atoms!

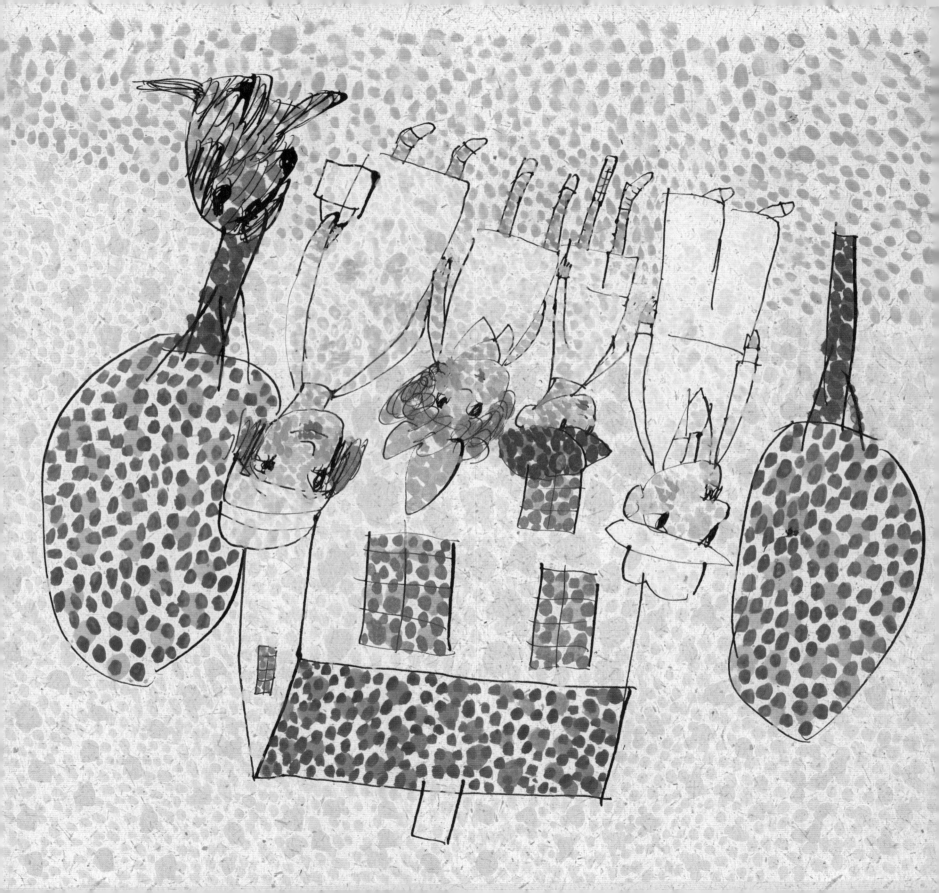

Then Albert thought about motion.

He realized that everything is always moving.
Moving through space, moving through time. Even sound asleep
we're moving, as our planet circles the sun, and our lives travel into
the future. Albert saw time and space as no one ever had before.

Albert wrote down his new ideas, put them into envelopes, and sent them to science magazines. The magazines printed everything Albert sent. He hoped that scientists and professors would be interested. And they were. Very interested indeed!

They asked Albert to come work with them and teach with them.

For the first time in his life, people started to say, "Albert is a genius!" Now Albert could spend all his days doing what he loved—imagining, wondering, figuring and thinking.

ALBERT Einstein is a genius!

Albert thought about very, very big things.

Like the size and shape of the entire universe.

He thought about very, very small things.

Like what goes on inside the atoms that everything is made of.

He thought about mysterious forces, like magnetism and gravity.

He discovered whole new ways to understand how all these things work.

Everywhere Albert went he would think and think. One of Albert's favorite thinking places was his little sailboat. He loved to let his mind wander as the wind blew him across the water.

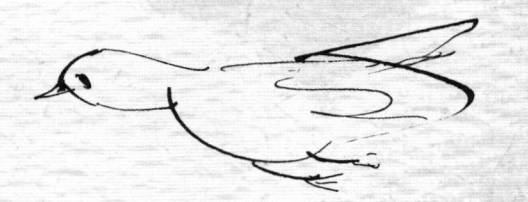

Sometimes, when Albert was having a tough time with a tricky problem, he would put it aside and play his violin.
Music made Albert happy. He said it helped him think better.

Albert even chose his clothes for thinking.
His favorites were his comfy, old saggy-baggy sweaters and pants.
And shoes without socks. He said now that he was grown up,
no one could tell him to put on his socks.

My feet
Are happier
without socks!

In the town where he lived, he became known for wandering around, deep in thought. Sometimes eating an ice-cream cone. Always recognizable with his long, wild hair, which by then had become quite white.

Everywhere Albert went he tried to figure out the secrets of the universe. And he never forgot about the beam of light that he rode so long ago in his imagination.

Albert figured out that no person, no thing, could ever zoom through space as fast as a beam of light.

He figured that if he could travel near the speed of light, crazy things would happen! Only minutes would pass for Albert,

while years and years went by for the rest of us!

This idea was so amazing, people didn't believe it at first, but scientists today have proven that it's true.

ALBERT EINSTEIN

Albert thought and figured until the very last minute of the very last day of his life. He asked questions never asked before. Found answers never found before. And dreamed up ideas never dreamt before.

Albert's ideas helped build spaceships and satellites that travel to the moon and beyond. His thinking helped us understand our universe as no one ever had before.

But still, Albert left us many big questions. Questions that scientists are working on today.

Questions that someday **you** may answer . . .
by wondering, thinking, and imagining.

Author's note

Albert Einstein was an extraordinary, fascinating person. I feel fortunate for the time I spent exploring his thrilling ideas and his intriguing universe while researching and writing this book. Einstein's life was so big and this book is so short, I couldn't fit everything in. But here are a few last important and interesting things I want to tell you about.

—J.B.

Einstein's Thought Experiments

One of Einstein's most remarkable talents was his ability to visualize experiments in his mind. Many of his ideas came to him first as images, and only later were turned into words and equations. Some of his greatest concepts started as what he called a *Gedankenexperiment*, or "thought experiment," in which he would imagine events happening in time and space. His visions were full of people, light, and moving objects. From these visualized scenarios, Einstein would come to whole new realizations about the workings of the universe.

Einstein's Playfulness and Laughter

Einstein loved jokes and clever, amusing tricks and sometimes even toys. He was in many ways as open and playful as a child, and adored his conversations with young children. People who spent time with him often commented on his booming laugh, his sparkling eyes, and his pure ability to enjoy life's little amusements and surprises. And children seemed to love him as much as he loved them.

$E=mc^2$

This famous and remarkable equation is one of Einstein's greatest legacies. In those few simple mathematical characters, Einstein described how even the teeniest, tiniest bits of matter can be turned into astoundingly huge amounts of power and energy. And that was something that people never, ever had imagined was possible.

The Atomic Bomb and Einstein's Pacifism

In a series of strange twists of life and fate, Einstein's discoveries about matter and energy were the foundational ideas that led other scientists to the invention of the atomic bomb. Einstein never wanted the atomic bomb to be used, ever. Einstein was a pacifist, a person who believes in peaceful ways to solve the world's problems, and thought wars were barbaric. He felt all war needed to end if mankind was to advance into the future.

Books about Einstein

There are hundreds of books written about Albert Einstein, and many that he wrote himself. To research this story, I read more than 50 of those books. A lot of reading! Here are a few of the most interesting and important ones.

Folsing, Albrecht. *Albert Einstein: A Biography*. New York: Penguin, 1998.

Hoffman, Banesh. *Creator and Rebel: Albert Einstein*. New York: Viking Press, 1972.

Isaacson, Walter. *Einstein: His Life and Universe*. New York: Simon & Schuster, 2008.

Pais, Abraham. *Subtle Is the Lord: The Science and the Life of Albert Einstein*. Oxford: Oxford University Press, 1982.

Schilpp, Paul Arthur, ed. *Albert Einstein: Philosopher-Scientist*. La Salle: Open Court, 1988.

I also recommend the Einstein Archives Online: www.alberteinstein.info.

Text © 2013 by Jennifer Berne.
Illustrations © 2013 by Vladimir Radunsky.

Library of Congress Cataloging-in-Publication Data

Berne, Jennifer.
On a beam of light: a story of Albert Einstein /
by Jennifer Berne ; illustrated by Vladimir
Radunsky.
     p. cm.
ISBN 978-0-8118-7235-5 (alk. paper)
1. Einstein, Albert, 1879–1955 — Juvenile literature.
2. Physicists — Biography — Juvenile literature.
I. Radunsky, Vladimir, ill. II. Title.
QC16.E5B437 2013
530.092 — dc22
[B]

                    2011004026

Book and cover design by Vladimir Radunsky.
Prepress by Katharina Gasterstadt.
Typeset in Didot.
The illustrations in this book were rendered
in goache, pen, and ink.

Manufactured in China.

Chronicle Books LLC
680 Second Street
San Francisco, California 94107

www.chroniclekids.com

Einstein's FAVORITE
bLUE CUP

Einstein's FAVORITE FORMULA

$$E = mc^2$$

Einstein's FAVORITE
violin And Bow

Einstein's FAVORITE
SHOES

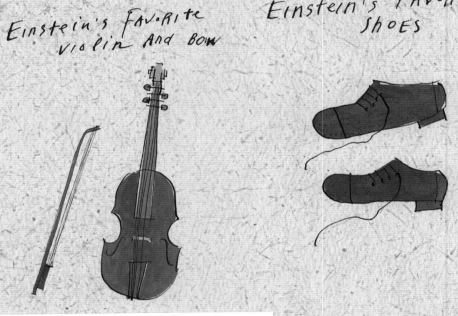

10 9 8 7 6 5 4 3 2 1